W9-BSQ-819

Better Than Church

by James H. Rutz

with

Gene Edwards

The SeedSowers
Christian Books Publishing House
Auburn, Maine 04212-3368

Copyright
1990
Printed in the United States of America
by James H. Rutz

First Edition: December, 1990
Second Edition: February, 1991
Third Edition: May, 1991
Open Church Ministries
1300 Adams, Bldg 8K
Costa Mesa, California 92626
This special limited edition revised and published by:
The SeedSowers
Christian Books Publishing House
P.O. Box 3368
Auburn, Maine 04212
ISBN 0-940232-46-4
Library of Congress Catalog Number: 91-76170

Introduction:
Ever Feel Like Quitting Church?

If you've ever felt lonely and unimportant in the church, there's a good reason: You *are* alone and unimportant.

From 11 to 12 Sunday, you're just another pretty face.

Though surrounded by others, you're cut off. It is custom that walls you off in your own space and silences your voice in the Sunday morning worship service.

Surrounded by an audience of trainee mutes, you can find it lonely as a solo trek across Antarctica... after you've eaten all the sled dogs.

The Sunday service would be exactly the same without you. You know that. Your impact on it is like an extra gallon of water going over Niagara Falls.

What's Wrong Here?

The heart of a church meeting today *is* the Sunday morning service, where the typical communication pattern is about as useful as a jello telephone.

No matter ·vhat you have on your heart—the greatest joy or deepest sorrow—you are not allowed to share it during the service. *Ever*.

Fellowship is confined to the foyer afterward, please. (Unless you've figured a way to fellowship with the back of someone else's head.) Try to talk, and the ushers will ush you out. Post hastily.

This, my friend, is *not* Biblical. St. Peter would have wept.

In fact, many of the early churches almost *demanded* you share something every week. They even expected you to *sing* for them. Even *solos!*

But now you can't say anything longer than "Hallelujah!"—if that. As a result, you are more of a spectator than a participant.

How did we ever get into such a fix? Well, **around A.D. 300, the church made the worst blunder in her history. We *voluntarily* decided to give up the three key freedoms that powered the early church to success:**

> **open worship**
> **open sharing**
> **open ministry**

Throughout Christendom, in the fourth century, men professionalized the local church and turned over Sunday services to the pros, leaving them to do almost everything.

Lay *men* found themselves stripped of initiative and power, like newly-captured slaves. Lay *women* were quietly relieved of what little responsibility and leadership they had. (By about 450 A.D., even the congregational singing faded to zip, as music was turned over to professional choirs of men and boys.)

The laity suddenly found Sunday worship to be more distant from their personal lives and daily concerns. They fell into Spectator Christianity, where loneliness doesn't end in a church gathering—it *starts* there.

The Key Malady

Today, at the beginning of the second millennium, we're still fighting the fallout from that massive mistake. Do any of these sound familiar?

1. apathy
2. shallowness
3. worldliness
4. failure to tithe
5. pastoral burnout
6. teenage dropouts
7. fear of evangelism
8. flabby self-discipline
9. maxed-out schedules
10. a chronic shortage of strong men.

I'm claiming that all of these maladies, and more, are caused mainly by one master malady: the closed meeting. In it laymen are passive observers while ministers are the overworked insiders.

The Reformation was a great start on fixing what was wrong with the church, but it fell far short in regard to structures and practice.

It succeeded marvelously in getting back to sound doctrine: *sola Scriptura* (placing the Bible over Church tradition), *sola gratia* (salvation by grace), and *sola fide* (through faith, not works).

But the Reformation never got us back to the first century pattern of meeting that we see in Paul's letters. It simply exchanged the priest for a minister and put a sermon in place of the Eucharist (communion). Thus the reformers left behind a matched set of migraines that would give St. Paul the yips.

The good news is that today *you* can finish the **Reformation. The ten problems just listed don't have to be solved one by one.** They are like a massive log jam that needs only one well-placed explosion to unsnarl the whole mess. By following first century guidelines, by opening the church to the rank and file, you can eventually:

1. Go from pew warmers to spiritual warriors.
2. Be part of a service so exciting no one wants to leave.
3. See marginal believers who quit meeting with other believers long ago (out of frustration or lack of interest) coming back to the Lord.[1]
4. See teenagers get excited about Jesus Christ.
5. See *men* return to your meetings.
6. Be one of many in the body of Christ

[1] NEW YORK (EP)—A significant number of "unchurched" Americans feel there is not enough emphasis on spiritual experience in the churches, according to a major research project conducted by George Gallup, Jr., for 30 denominations and religious organizations.

At a news conference at the Interchurch Center, the pollster commented that "more of the unchurched than the churched have had a sudden religious experience. They're all charged up, with with no place to go."

Dr. Gallup noted that a key criticism of the unchurched in regard to religious institutions is that "Churches have lost the spiritual part of religion." About one of every five unchurched persons who indicated they had "problems" with churches checked a statement which said, "I wanted deeper spiritual meaning than I found in the church or synagogue."

A summary report indicated...41 per cent unchurched would project to approximately 61 million [U.S.] adults. 6/24/78 who experience pure, uplifting worship (as in Revelation 4 and 5) along with deep, lasting friendships.

7. Watch the church become soul-winners.
8. End the rat race of unfocused church activities that is sapping the drive of God's people.
9. Discover a whole new feeling of love toward God's people.

This list probably strikes you as wishful thinking. I think I know why: because the last time a majority of our churches were successful in most of these nine areas, Nero was burning Christians to light his garden at night.

Actually, that's unfair. There have been—and are now—many churches that have made most of these changes. However, most of these are overseas, purified by persecution.

In any case, the world is now careening rapidly toward a whole new political, economic, and spiritual order. The fate of hundreds of millions of souls hangs on whether or not the church is able to gear up and capture the day.

78 Leaking Buckets

By latest count, there are 78 plans for world evangelization created by existing churches (and parachurch organizations), each with a budget over $100 million dollars per decade. Twenty-one of them expect to finish the job by the year 2000.[2]

---

[2] David Barrett and James Reapsome, *Seven Hundred Plans to Evangelize the World* (Birmingham, AL: New Hope), $6.95.

To the best of my knowledge, all of them are designed to dump their new converts into the same old closed-church patterns that perpetuate the same old leaky-bucket problems. The plans don't take into account the basic problem: The basis of our operations, the church, is dynamically flawed. Yes, after all these centuries: still flawed.

It's time to reopen our meetings. Wouldn't you say 1700 years is long enough?

1

The Disastrous Success of A.D. 300:
How the Church
Managed to Hog-Tie Itself

A funny thing happened on the way to the Lord's return: In the fourth century, the church's wheels fell off.

Until then, it had looked like the gospel would reach the uttermost parts at chariot race speed. Or at least before McDonald's did.

No such luck. Around A.D. 300, the church made the biggest blunder in its history, and we crashed like an Indy 500 racer with a stuck throttle and a full tank of gas.

Hardly anyone knows about this blunder today except scholars (who know all about it, but discuss it just among themselves). And yet the effects were disastrous:

- Laymen lost the three key freedoms that had fueled the rapid growth of the church: *open worship, open sharing, and open ministry.*
- The church degenerated from an army, (or family) into an audience—*overnight* in some places!
- Evangelism slowed to a crawl. Then to

an ooze.

- Church leaders got the bright idea of diversifying into politics, and took over whole governments. We now remember this period as the, uh, *Dark Ages*.

Where Did We Go Wrong?

Within thirty years of Christ's ascension, the gospel was being preached in every outpost of the Roman Empire.

Unencumbered by church buildings, mortgages, committees, staff salaries, and conflicts between choir rehearsal and church softball team practice, the "followers of the Way" blazed a trail of stunning successes.

The church grew in the first three centuries, thriving on hard times and persecution.

- In hard times, the church's strong grass-roots mutual-assistance charities held everyone together.
- In persecution, the government sharply defined the church by pushing believers together. The act of taking a stand for Christ strengthened each man, woman, and child.

What was their secret? First the presence of the living God in their hearts. Second, the weekly gathering of the body of believers in homes, an informal and often-boisterous affair with a full-on meal, not just a polite ceremony with an itty bitty breadcrumb and a thimbleful of Welch's grape juice.

At that weekly get-together, everyone was the star of the show, everyone was needed. Spirits were lifted, problems solved, hurts healed, hearts fed, and the Lord of lords spoke to every soul. But the *whoopee!* part of the meeting, the "love-feast" (Jude 12), resembled a cross between a Super Bowl victory celebration and a frat party (with a few cups of wine instead of a keg of suds).[3]

From our vantage point today, it looks as if they had an unbeatable thing going. A sure-fire, run-away, free-wheeling style of church that was gobbling up Satan's territory like a giant pac-man.

Why then, did the roaring success of the early days fade? When did we cool off?

Well, as we grew larger and more popular, our feeling of being a distinct family waned. In a well-churched city, it's hard to think of everybody as a brother or sister in the Lord. "Us vs. Them" psychology doesn't work when almost everyone is us. The church became less a revolutionary band and more of a static establishment.

Eloquent preachers began to attract large followings.

The final straw came in 313, when Emperor Constantine I issued the *Edict of Milan,* officially tolerating the church and ending the persecutions. Church leaders from popes to local bishops got involved with the government. Many even became government officials. At that time it looked like a good idea. ("Hey, we won! Now we can take over!")

---

[3]As Tony Campolo overstates in his latest book, *The Kingdom of God is a Party:* "The pharisees gave him a hard time because Jesus was always going to parties with publicans, tax collectors and with whores. But Jesus had in mind a church that would throw parties for people who never went to parties, people who are left out."

As it turned out, though, it was a lousy idea. Our top leaders drifted astray on a long, long power trip and let their flocks wander.

The Constantine Fiasco

But what really killed us was the bricks.

In the biggest blunder in her history, the church began constructing lots of buildings, displacing the living rooms, catacombs and forest glens—and ending forever the warm, precious, meetings in someone's living room.

Modeled after the Roman forums, the new buildings held hundreds of Christians. Of course, you can't have intimate, easy interaction with that size of crowd. So from the first Sunday it opened, a new sanctuary put limits on free expression. The new crib strangled the baby.

Imagine you were living in that time:

- You may have felt at ease confessing a sin to a couple of dozen friends over at Josephus and Johanna's (or let's call them Joe and Jane). But in front of five hundred strangers? Whoa!
- If God taught you something this week and it lay strongly on your heart, you wouldn't hesitate to stand up and spend ten minutes sharing it in Joe and Jane's living room. But in the new hall, with a ritual, where sharing would disrupt the entire meeting? Forget it!
- Over at Joe and Jane's, everybody got into the act in the worship time. You were able to praise the Lord from your heart—again and again as you felt led.

It was the most meaningful and healing moment of your week. But in today's church building? Take a number!

I could go on, but you get the idea. Open meetings became difficult, if not impossible. Closed meetings took over. All speaking became centralized in a pulpit. Order *was* maintained. (Again, it seemed like a good idea at the time.)

At Joe and Jane's, you were a participant. Today, you're a spectator. A passive listener. A blip.

At first you don't mind it. the change is all so exciting. And being with 500 believers at once—wow! Paradise! Not until years later does it dawn on you that you've been turned into a pew potato.

But now, with 1,000 eyes focused on the pulpit, the man behind it *has become extremely important.* He's very, very good, of course—probably the best speaker in the area. His warmth and wisdom and skill defuse any latent objections to the new state of affairs. Certainly, his polished sermons beat the sandals off the impromptu teachings you used to hear—and give—at Joe and Jane's.

So it doesn't take long before every local church from London to Alexandria has its own building and its own professional Christian standing up in front every Sunday, doing the talking. Eventually, the love-feasts get so big and rowdy that they're banned.

No prophet or leader comes to the fore to decry the passing of the house church or condemning the new diversion of church funds into real estate development. No one of any note questions taking initiative away from ordinary believers and bestowing it upon the new priesthood class.

And no one points out that the Holy Scriptures do not sanction any of this.

Paradise Lost

All the major problems of the church today—other than sin—can be traced back 1700 years, to when the church became an audience.

When we switched from living rooms to church buildings and professionally staffed the local church, we lost all momentum. The local church became weak and cold.

Non-priests were termed "laymen," a word not even found in the Bible (for good reason). As a layman in the worship service, you no longer approached God directly. The priest did so on your behalf. And thus did a real estate problem turn into a doctrinal problem. The priesthood of the believer was lost.

The Scripture was taken from the hands of the layman and given to the priest. (If you're not allowed to decide what it means, why bother to read it?)

With the Scriptures out of the hands of the people, the priesthood was free to play with it. For a thousand years, cloistered monks lovingly piled theological baggage atop the Bible until, by the time of Luther, hardly a layman in Europe knew the all-important meaning of "justification by faith."

Without the Scriptures to lift them out of the mud, laymen turned into serfs in the feudalism of the Dark Ages.

Ironically, in that darkness the only candle of hope and upward mobility was the church. Becoming a priest was the only way out of oblivion. We often laud the medieval church for providing this escape hatch from the pit; we should remember, though, that the

6

church dug that pit.

The Road to Ruin

The early church had so much success and momentum that they should logically have evangelized everyone from Turkey to Tokyo by A.D. 600.

Many historians say the problem was that believers felt disillusioned when Christ didn't return right away. Well, we now have nineteen centuries of "disillusionment," and we're the biggest religion in the world. What really went haywire?

As I said, the church got so big and popular that it could erect its own buildings. Unfortunately, *this solved a long-standing problem that should have been left standing: Whenever a healthy house-church got too big for its living room, it had to split—into two living rooms.* New leadership was thus always being sucked upward through the ranks.

But when church buildings began to sprout across the Empire, congregations no longer had to face the awkward anguish of who got to stay in an established house meeting and who had to split off with the nobodies. Everybody stayed with everybody. Heavenly!

Trouble is, sharing and intimacy was difficult in a crowd of 500. And the big crowds put a premium on eloquence. So the stuttering new converts began to stay in their shells. Anonymity replaced fellowship. Communication during meetings began to be dominated by the few who could read and to those who had access to books: In the end, that meant *priests.* The laity, citizens of a long-crumbling Roman empire, were turned into spiritual eunuchs and lost the strength the empire needed so desperately at that time. By 476 Rome fell for the last time, and the church led the way into the Dark Ages.[4]

The 2/3 Reformation

A thousand tear-stained years later, Luther, Calvin & Co. began picking up the pieces.

They put Christian theology back together.

They also worked a little—too little—on the church's practices and functions, and got about half of them glued back together. Maybe two-thirds. Excellent work, as far as it went. The best "fixit" job since Nehemiah.

But they couldn't do everything. Rome wasn't unbuilt in a day. So the Puritans had to pick up some more pieces. In the 18th century, the Wesleys picked up some more. In the 19th century, the revivalists and missionaries picked up more.

But there's still a gigantic hole in the church. **The "priesthood of the believer," the central goal of the Reformation, has been restored only** *theologically*... **not practically. It still exists mainly on paper.** *In very important ways, our churches remain closed to laymen.*

Between clergy and laity there is still a big, uncrossable gap—academic, professional, and liturgical.

For example:

- Even though we acknowledge the common saying, *"Everyone has at least one sermon in him,"* almost no one is ever encouraged or even allowed to

---

[4] As I see it, when large sanctuaries sprang up, sitting and listening to an eloquent orator portray the glories of God and the Christian life proved to be easier and more popular than trying to be one of 500 active participants.

8

deliver that *one* sermon. This practice is a horrendous exercise in quenching the Spirit. It frosts me that the "one sermon" in the heart of a faithful dentist or truck driver or engineer should forever be deemed less worthwhile than any of the two thousand sermons in the lifetime of a pastor.

- We don't allow laymen to mature into ministers. Jesus and Paul believed in on-the-job training; we put our faith in seminaries. Most of the church is too watery to formulate and enforce Biblical standards for full-time body ministry.
- We almost idolize schools and their graduates. Their lecterns are baptized as pulpits, lectures become sermons, students are parishioners, and degrees are, well, required...from world-approved institutions. But even in college, if you sit still for seven years, they'll give you a Ph.D. and let you stand up and do all the talking.

  In church, you can sit for seventy years and never get to say a peep. Worse, you'll be conditioned to be *afraid* to peep. The system is designed to be static!
- Question: How can a minister "equip the saints for the work of the ministry" when he holds a monopoly on so much of that work? Nonetheless, this *is* the

9

pastor's job description. So he lives
with a blizzard of details.

Laymen today have regained the **Word** of God,
but not the **work** of God. The priesthood of the believer has been restored *de jure,* not *de facto*.

The very earliest Christians had plenty of problems, but the pastor-centered church wasn't one of
them. Those churches, and the gatherings of God's
people, were people-led. The burden of God's work
was spread like dew on the prairie.

How Can We See These Things Happen Again?

We can begin by opening up the meetings of the
church, granting full participation rites to all those nice
folks taking up pew space on Sunday morning. In
other words, unlock the church.

We commonly say we're "participating" in a service when actually we're mostly just watching. Let's be
clear on this distinction. For example, think of a pro
baseball game. Do they let us spectators run out on the
field and play? No way. We lack the skill.

Participants actually affect the outcome. Better
you and I should watch in baseball, but *participate* in
church.

2

Sure, It's a Worship Service--
Says So Right Here in the Bulletin

The early church managed the prodigious feat of being healthy without a King James Bible. Or Christian TV. Or seminaries or Calvin's *Institutes* or Sunday school buses or parachurch organizations, or even a church building.

The secret of their success? Every week, believers gathered for a catch-all meeting where they participated and worshiped God heart to heart.

In that intimate communion, they gathered enormous strength directly from the Holy Spirit and shed the thousand-and-one cares that weigh upon the human heart. Thus transformed, they dispersed as witnesses.

That was the pattern. In, out...in, out. As healthful as breathing.

Today's "worship" services, however, produce precious little actual worship in the strict sense: praise and worship that is conceived and spoken by individuals.

The great A.W. Tozer said that worship is "the missing jewel of the evangelical church." Precisely. Except for a few minutes of group singing, the believer normally has no chance to express his adoration and worship, to make that vital, creature-to-Creator contact. He can only listen to a leader doing these things on his behalf. Worship is almost wholly vicarious for those of us in the pews.

Charismatic and Pentecostal churches do allow for two or three messages in tongues, interpretations, prophecies, or "words of knowledge." But these are usually given by the more advanced members, with beginners too intimidated to try. Moreover, the emphasis in these services is on guidance (a message *from* God), not worship directed *toward* God, and not fellowship *with* God.

You'll find pure worship in Revelation 4 and 5. But when it's brought into a Sunday service, it's always in *music* or *responsive readings*. Sam and Sue Christian are never allowed to choose such words and speak them from their hearts to God.

This may help to explain why the typical North American who claims to be born again can't even name the gospels and has all the spiritual depth of a birdbath.

What to Do About It

I suggest three steps.
1. Sharpen everyone's vision and thirst for involvement in worship.
   Work toward meetings with open participation and worship. (You may wish to review material like Ray Stedman's classic *Body Life*.) [5]

----

[5] Regal Books (1979), $6.95.

2. Gather to truly function as a body.
Give much of the entire meeting to a
body life format.[6]
Lengthen your meeting if you need to.
Rearrange it if you wish.
3. Enable each person to actually start
making his own unique, maximum
contribution to the meeting.
Just knowing you *should* participate in
this manner will not suffice for everyone. Some things we learn only by
doing. Some people learn slowly; a
certain amount of hand-holding *will* be
needed. Bank on it.

It will take time to warm up to an open meeting.
But once Christians get into it, you've got a cannon-
ball. They will not want to stop.

I was once in a large, *stand-up* prayer meeting

---

[6] As background information, you may be interested to know
that there already exists a loosely-structured denomination, called
by outsiders the Plymouth Brethren, that offers unstructured wor-
ship/communion services. In the U.S. and Canada, they have
over 1200 mostly-small assemblies that meet in low-key "gospel halls" or "Bible chapels." The PBs are arguably the most
orthodox of all evangelical denominations in their worship practices. Why, then, have they not come to dominate the church
scene? Among several factors, I would note that they never allow women to speak in the services, and PB sermons, being
impromptu, are seldom the rich, satisfying, highly-illustrated
masterpieces you can find in other churches. In the face of
oppostion, however, the PBs have proven to be the most resilient
denomination of all. They have thrived in China, where there are
now possibly 30 to 50 million believers; and in the Soviet Union,
a great many of the churches officially lumped together as
"Baptist" are actually P.B.

where we simply changed the ground rules to: "Use single-sentence prayers and finish each topic before you move on." Afterward, we all thought we'd prayed 15 or 20 minutes, but it was an hour! No one could believe it.

Participation makes your meeting a little longer, but it adds oceans of joy and excitement and spiritual growth, with deep calling unto deep. On the road to depth and maturity, you can't skip the infancy stage; before you begin to conquer principalities, you have to learn to say, "Abba, Father."

Your people will remain loyal to your group because they can't find true worship in that megachurch across town or that super-friendly church down the road. Why? Worship is like breathing—*exhaling* as well as *inhaling*. And most churches forbid exhaling!

Worship, Band-aids, and Jammed Schedules

How did the primitive church ever make it without Sunday school?... or music committees?... or high school ski conferences?... or divorce recovery workshops?

Answer: Open meetings and close-knit experience met most all needs.

But today's worshipless worship services, with their lack of community, leave a vacuum. Hence the smorgasbord approach: activities designed to meet a specific felt need, to make up for the absence of something a full-orbed, open service could likely do.

But those activities are not usually part of a strategy to reach the world or give the devil a splitting headache. They are knee-jerk reactions, *ad-hoc* solutions.

Take Sunday school for an example. God's plan for religious education is *Dad*. It's a 4000-year-old plan that's worked like a watch since the days of Abraham. But if your weekly gathering doesn't equip Dad to open his mouth—well, that is why the church invented Sunday school. (Programming Dad would be easier.)

Your three dozen programs were launched as mechanisms to fill needs. It's a Band-Aid system.

Of course, the system does nuke your free time and imprison you behind a stained-glass curtain.

As ad-hoc activities proliferate, it becomes impossible to maintain a sharp focus. A church may reach what Tom Sine *(The Mustard Seed Conspiracy)* calls a state of "chronic randomness," doing forty things that as a whole are less than the sum of their parts.

Solution strategy: Rather than relying on programs designed to fill holes or meet isolated needs, go for an integrated menu of high-stakes meetings that directly transform hearts and pound the gates of Hell into splinters. Live dangerously, as the apostles did.

Give up the predictability and safety of a rigid, fully-programmed service. Step out in faith and learn to function as a body, in a body. You don't need to do anything fancy.

Just have a back-to-basics meeting that allows for open worship and open sharing.

3

Sharing Time:
When the Church Lights Up
Like a Christmas Tree

I used to attend a friendly, growing church, with a minister who was loved by even the worst grouch.

But though it was a model church in many ways, nothing much ever happened inside me. "Worship" services were actually a warm-hearted lecture series, plus songs and offering. Almost never was I allowed to participate, except as the 387th voice in a song.

If I'd never shown up, my absence would have been like a missing spoonful of sand from the Arabian desert. Without me, not one syllable would have changed—and that's about how significant I felt. Fact is, that's how significant I was. So I drifted away.

In a typical church there is no opportunity for people to share their grief or joy or even the deepest needs of their lives. They may die without anyone in church knowing the burning hopes and fears in their hearts—the "staff" always has the spotlight.

It's the closed-church *system* that consigns everyone to the role of a mute non-person, a face without a voice or heart.

You would think the Holy Spirit would have made

a dent in this dreadful system by now. But no, most Christians (including many in the ministry) seem allergic to the free-form, overflowing fellowship that open sharing can create.

I've been in a number of churches where opening the meeting saw a torrent of pent-up emotions, confessions, praises, tears, new commitments, lumpy throats—and wide-eyed amazement. But of course it's inherently unplanned (therefore "out of control"), so the pastor quickly reverted back to the closed format. I've just never understood this.

The Impossible Situation

When response, participation and sharing are forbidden till the service is over, what can you expect?

And it really is forbidden. Suppose, for instance, some gent pops up in the middle of the sermon next Sunday and says,

> "Hey, great point! The Lord's been teaching me a lot about that lately. In fact, this past week I experienced an amazing example of what you just described. On Tuesday morning..."

The nearest usher will invite him to hit the bricks. Straightway and forthwith. The #1 rule for a closed, non-participatory service is, "Siddown and shuddup."

Yes, they're supposed to respond wholeheartedly to the sermon ... but only *after* they go home and get down to real life!

Things were different in days of yore, when the church of Jesus Christ was turning Rome on its imperial ear. Men were free to obey the promptings of the Holy Spirit and speak up when they had something to say. They were born running—talking in church and witnessing outside it. And in the space of three centuries, they had reached quite a bit of the known world. Without even any *Four Laws* booklets.

That shows they were better witnesses than most Christians today. And why? Because the meetings didn't stifle them. It conditioned them to communicate their faith. Meetings were different then. Livelier. More off-the-wall. We don't have many specifics about what they looked like, but we do have a *few*. Such as these...

Three Clues

1. "When you come together, **everyone** has something to contribute: a hymn, or a word of instruction, a revelation, a tongue or an interpretation...you can all prophesy in turn..."
   Meetings in Corinth were a free-for-all, so Paul was telling them to act more Presbyterian. But notice: He did endorse individual contributions by everyone.
2. "While they were worshiping the Lord and fasting, the holy Spirit said, 'Set apart for me Barnabas and Saul...'"
   This couldn't happen in the church today! Our worship patterns don't allow it, and we don't often do fasts. Missionaries in our age get their calls straight from God, then spend eons convincing supporters they did.
3. "Speak to *one another* with psalms, hymns, and spiritual songs..." Precisely what does "one another" mean?

18

Group singing? Hardly! Tertullian tells us what it meant in his day:

"In our Christian meetings we have plenty of songs, verses, sentences and proverbs. [obviously individual] After hand-washing and bringing in the lights, each Christian is asked to stand forth and sing, as best he can, a hymn to God, either of his own composing, or one from the Holy Scriptures.

Try that next Sunday!

In Tertullian's time (A.D. 160-230) there were many assemblies that were interactive powerhouses, not audiences. So how, then, did St. Murphy's Law derail the church from such a fast track?

Simple. By abandoning house-churches, we ran afoul of a Murphy corollary, Gall's *Non-Additivity Theorem:*

A Large System, Produced by Expanding the Dimensions of a Smaller System, Does Not Behave Like the Smaller System.

The Nuts and Bolts of Sharing

Try to envision being in a future participatory gathering of a body of believers. Here are some of the ingredients you might see:

- Individual praise and worship
- Thanksgiving and testimony
- Confession
- Silent meditation
- Encouragement and cheer by others
- Original poetry and song
- Intercession

- Sharing of God's lessons learned
- Sharing of needs
- On-the-spot decision-making and commitments

This is the free mode of body life. Imagine...

- The excitement of God's people praying for each other and bearing one another's heavy loads;
- The enrichment and joy of hearing what God has been doing in different families;
- The thrill of seeing former fraidy-cats stand and worship the Lord, praising Him for who He is and what He's done;
- The added meaning in knowing that some of the hymns and readings came from the pens of believers sitting around you.

Sharing Kills Apathy

One problem you'll never have to worry about in an open gathering is apathy.

Apathy is totally impossible when you're dodging bullets. Or when you're halfway across a high wire. Or when the center snaps you the ball, and a very serious-looking 6'8" gentleman rips open the line and lunges for your throat.

The common element here is involvement. And that's the solution to apathy: total involvement. When you can look around and see scores of people who are committed to sharing your burden, you are in the middle of total involvement.

The vastly increased involvement that fellowship

and sharing entail obliterates apathy.

As with open worship time, the key is a few believers breaking the ice for a few weeks.

Apathy is impossible when you're:

- standing in the meeting, praying for the brother beside you who has just been diagnosed as having cancer;
- asking for prayer about getting a job to replace the one you just lost Friday;
- volunteering to stay with a sick kid someone just told about.[7]

Like the open-worship period, the open sharing will add a few minutes to the meeting. In the USSR, Christians normally meet for nearly three hours, and they pack'em in like caviar. They must know something!

Eliminate Teen Dropout

Teenagers are our most wasted resource.

They drop out at eighteen and don't come back until twenty-eight (with spouse and baby in tow).

At eighteen, they're 95% ready to function as adults. But no one wants to take them seriously, even in the body of Christ. So they drift off.

Solution: Make sure they're integrated into the open-format time from the very first meeting.

They are needed and wanted; just show them how to blend in with what God is doing thematically. They'll eat it up. Adults might feel patronized, but for teens, it's rite-of-passage stuff, like keys to the car. This is their big chance to become functional adults, in

---

[7] In a large sanctuary, fellowship usually requires roving mikes and two or three runners to tote them.

one giant step. (Do you know what Napoleon said was the high point of his life? His first communion as a youth.)

Once integrated, teens will seldom drop out. Younger ones will begin to mature nicely. Older ones will slide right into their adult role—some of them even before age eighteen. (The great thing about church life is, nobody checks your I.D. card to see how old you are.)

4

Open Ministry:
The Only Way We'll Ever
Get the Job Done

The category of "layman" (and laywoman) needs to be scratched.

Because it is:

1. **Unscriptural.** In the Greek, "laos" (layman) simply means "people." It has nothing to do with not being in the ministry.
2. **Dead wrong.** If you're an earnest Christian, you *have* a ministry. (1 Cor. 12:7, 11, 13, 27)
3. **Negative.** It defines you by what you *aren't*.
4. **Offensive.** The connotations of layman are in the same ballpark as peon, peasant, amateur, yokel, and the great unwashed.

This is a heavy point. You must realize that although you may not make your living at it, you *are* a minister of the gospel.

A ministry is simply the sphere in which you function as a believer. And you *do* have a spiritual ministry. You do! You do! You do!

The Church with No Laymen

In a big old house on embassy row in Washington, D.C., you'll find a congregation called the Church of the Saviour, a small Presbyterian church that has been written up in many magazines and several books.[8]

They wouldn't claim to be perfect, but they sure do a lot of things right. So far, they've split off eight new congregations in order to remain small. And aspiring members must wait up to two years before acceptance—including fifty-five weeks of classes! Before Constantine, converts often had quite a wait before they could "join" a church, but in this era, Church of the Saviour stands out like a plaid pig.

Their secret of success is that nobody can join without also joining one of their groups of about four to eight people.

Each group has a double focus. First, it has a task. Groups form when someone feels led to undertake a mission or shoulder a responsibility. He or she issues a call for other members to join in the new task; if enough respond, the group begins. That is the *outward* focus.

Second, the group meets once a week. Everyone keeps a spiritual journal. They share their personal progress and problems, and support each other. That is the *inward* focus.

Laminating the inward and outward is very, very smart. It enables them to avoid extremes: (a) the *hollowness* of a works-oriented group and (b) the *self-centered* introspection of a talk group.

---

[8] The best two are by Elizabeth O'Connor: *Call to Commitment* ($7.95) and her later *Journey Inward, Journey Outward* ($8.95), both from Harper & Row.

Now, any healthy church will eventually help its members find a ministry and achieve inner growth. But Church of the Saviour, by *requiring* you to find a fellowship-ministry upon joining, has it down to a fine art. If a layman is someone *not* in ministry, then it's fair to say *that congregation* has no laymen!

Ministry Starts at the Heart of the Church

With wide variations, the adventure toward an open church will include:

1. Commitment and Preparing. We *will* have an open meeting.
2. Participating in something called "body life." Eating together, "bearing one another's burdens." Picnics. Meetings to learn to sing together.

And much more. Although the worship service is an end in itself, it should lead to other expressions.

Deep involvement has to start at zero hour at Square One with a real-life, acted-out, spoken, functional acceptance into the innermost heart of the meeting.

In fewer words, **we absolutely must let each believer take full part in the heart of church life by speaking words of his own.** (Try to imagine a home where only the father could talk, and the mother and kids could only chant in unison.)

The Power of Open Ministry

In addition to an open worship meeting and body life, make sure your people see the big picture, the fact that ministry is now for everyone. In fact, God sometimes brings challenges that require the whole flock to pull together.

For instance, from 1961 to 1979, when many Christian leaders were being held as prisoners in China, Pastor M.Y. Chan worked in a night soil pit.

That means he spent six to eight hours a day standing in human excrement with no protection, filling buckets with waste to be spread on fields as fertilizer. His huge prison camp in Kiangsu province had four main latrine areas, and they all drained into one horrendous hellhole where he stood every day in sludge sometimes up to his waist.

Because his church knew of his plight and stood with him, he survived those 18-1/2 years without one sick day! Moreover, the people of that body witnessed like tigers and grew from 300 to 5,000 during his absence!

Now 58, he has churches in twenty locations, each with about a thousand believers. The church in China has learned how to function without their pastors—by involving everyone in open ministry.

Despite the fact that 325,800 Christians have been martyred per average recent year,[9] there are about 23,000 *new* Christians in mainland China *every day*—a growth rate about six times higher than the country itself!

We will all be strengthened by the fact that we are getting regular practice in proclaiming the whole counsel of God.

In the dark and middle ages, the only guy in church worth listening to was the only one who could read. But today in North America we have nearly full literacy and a crying need to widen our "resource

---

[9] From a conversation with David Barrett, the leading authority in that area.

base." That means *participation*. In a body of two hundred, for example, we can multiply our resources 20,000% simply by not holding people back any longer!

What happens when a man sits in a pew for fifty years? He gets thoroughly programmed, but only on his input circuit. He opens his mouth to witness, and—wonder of wonders—nothing comes out. He scratches his head and says, "Darn! I *know* all that stuff."

However, after a few months of participation, he will have some practice using his *output* circuit. Evangelism will come more easily. And if he has a *knack* for evangelism, his entire life will take on new meaning. He will bloom like a hillside of edelweiss.

5

It's Time to Reopen the Church

The time has come to end our 1700-year experiment in spectator Christianity.

Like a doting parent, God the Father is glad to take whatever He can get in the way of worship, but I'm here to tell you He'd be a whole lot happier if Sam Christian were allowed to stand to his feet in a meeting and say, "I love you, Lord. You mean everything to me."

What harm could come from that?

I live for the day when Sue Christian can stand up and tell how the Lord changed her life this week. Would the steeple be struck by fire from Heaven if a woman were to put in a good word for the Lord in a meeting?

Why can't we simply be a family together—God and His kids—doing what good families do: sharing their hearts and lives?

We don't need to get better at what we presently do on Sunday. We're already past masters at singing and at listening to sermons and announcements.

What we desperately need is to *do* something different and *be* something different. We need to learn to interact in depth with God and each other. In *that,* we're still in kindergarten.

A New Track Record: 0 to 65 in 90 Years

We can no longer afford present church customs and patterns. Present-day practices turn Christians into ineffectual wimps. We have to start behaving like men again, not standing around and waiting till asked to do something.

Why change now? Because the King of Heaven sets the pace, and His pace is jumping toward the moon. For instance, between 1980 and 1990, the percentage of the world's people who are unevangelized plummeted by 8.0%[10]

Amazing!

And yet 65 countries are now closed to all foreign missionaries (up from nearly **zero** in 1900) and about four more close each year, forcing us now to launch a massive tentmaker strategy. The Holy Spirit would like to send several families in your gathering abroad as tentmakers within the next twelve months.[11] Believe it!

You now know what an open church can accomplish. Business as usual won't do in your life anymore. I dare you turn back and forget you ever read all this...even if you wanted to! You must go forward.

---

[10]*Pulse,* March 23, 1990, p.1

[11] Global Opportunities (1600 Elizabeth, Pasadena, CA 91104, phone 818-398-2393) has 105,000 overseas, secular job openings on computer. For a very modest fee, they will match up a mission-minded Christian with exactly the kind of job he desires.

Pray

Spearhead the effort to open the church. And pray. But don't bother to ask God to clear the problems out of the path. That job belongs to you, pilgrim! Ask Him, rather, for three things: wisdom, power, and love.

Also, it would be very smart to ask for at least one kindred spirit to pray with and dream with. Lone Rangers don't get very far in the restoration business.

Whatever you do, don't let your efforts create friction. Keep it friendly! Keep it brotherly! Concentrate on the benefits of open meetings, the closer fellowship, growing, and learning. A you-versus-them scenario is the *last* thing you'll want.

The Impossible is Now Possible

Do all the high goals herein sound unrealistic to you? Under the status quo, they would be. But remember, we're talking about a revolution in how we meet that could transform people like a cold shower. There won't be many spiritual blobs who show up once a week, meet, and then vanish. God's people will be people of *action*. Concerned *participants!* Powerful, loving disciples who are taking their places as leaders in the battle force under the Commander of the Armies of Heaven.

So free yourself from deadening, unscriptural practices and make the Lord Jesus Christ the heart of the meeting—not just its titular head!

Start Today

Surely at some point in your life you've been in on at least one cottage prayer meeting or some informal gathering where the atmosphere was hushed and electric with the presence of God, where time stood still and people's whole lives were changed just by being there.

That's the sort of experience within your reach. It happens when you begin to be involved with people in open interaction and true worship. It happened in the primitive church, it has happened to me, and it can happen to you.

An open church will revive and transform like nothing else you can name. Your life will change gears, too.

Start the wheels rolling *now*. (Sharing this book with others is a good place to begin.)

In any case, do *something!* If you're like most harried believers, it's now or never.

6

Suddenly, the Battlefield Has Changed--and We're Not Prepared

Ever since Babel, the world has been splintered.

But since November 9, 1989, when the Berlin Wall opened, the pieces are being drawn together again by an Unseen Hand—with hair-raising speed and force.

We are living in the **first-ever** worldwide *kairos,* a God-driven time of crisis when the foundation of society is shifting beneath our feet.

The three bases of society are government, economics, and culture (which hinges on religion).

For the first time ever, mankind is reaching a consensus on its form of *government:* representative, multi-party democracy.

Mankind is reaching a consensus on its form of *economy:* free markets.

Soon there will be a consensus on the world's culture. Right now, though, it's still up for grabs. The only four worldwide religious forces capable of doing this are Islam, the New Age, Humanism, and Christianity. Here are the main factors working for and against each of them:

1. **Islam**

   Against: It's dictatorial, which puts it

on a collision course with free markets, free voting, and a high-tech communications web that transmits doubt, decadence, and pluralism directly from satellites to Muslim TV sets.

For: Islam is probably our #1 competition because it has such a strong hold on its people.

2. **New Age**

Against: Although the New Age is aided by TV and Hollywood, it lacks a driving organizational force. Also, it's based on Hinduism, which has never accomplished anything.

For: It's one of Satan's new projects.

3. **Humanism**

Against: Secular humanism is doomed because it has tried and failed even in its fleshed-out, full-dress form, Communism.

For: It remains the incumbent culture of the West—with the incumbent's advantages.

4. **Christianity**

Against: That leaves us chickens. You and me. Plus half a billion other Great Commission Christians.[12] Unfortunately, any study of church history strongly reminds us of Pogo's famous

---

[12] "Great Commission Christians" is a handy new phrase from the Statistics Task Force of the Lausanne Committee for World Evangelization. The estimate of 500 million is by Barrett, and Ralph Winter of the Center for World Mission.

conclusion, "We have met the enemy, and he is us."

For: If God be for us, who can be against us? (And you can quote me on that.)

The battle has shifted gears. It's now a battle for the entire planet's faith. There will be heavy casualties. (Barrett projects 500,000 Christian martyrs a year by 2000.)[13] We must get our act together and prepare the church for action or suffer badly for our unwillingness to discern God's hand in this kairos.

Why might we suffer? Partly because the blood of many martyrs may be required to crack the Muslim curtain. But mostly because we're not ready to handle the challenges of rapid growth.

The closed church system is so slow-moving that it takes years to prepare one person for ministry. Compare that to Paul's record of creating viable churches from scratch throughout Galatia, Asia, Achaia, and Macedonia between A.D. 47 and 57,...about ten years! With no New Testament (which he was busy writing).[14]

When God Strikes, Get Ready for Action

Russia was never exactly famous as an evangelical hot spot. But thanks to Mr. Marx, it is now! (So there's something to be said for dialectical materialism after all: the best appetizer for Christian truth ever invented.)

---

[13] David Barrett, *Cosmos, Chaos, and Gospel: A Chronology of World Evangelization from Creation to New Creation (1987).*

[14] If you think the comparison unfair, see Roland Allen's *Missionary Methods: St. Paul's or Ours?* (Eerdmans, $5.95).

The crumbling Soviet empire has quickly turned into an overwhelmingly huge, red-hot mission field which is so vast that the Western church hardly knows where to start. The Macedonian calls are reverberating like a 100,000-voice choir.

And let's hear it for Chairman Mao, without whom China would have remained the impenetrable morass that buffaloed missionaries for eighty-five years. Although Mao slaughtered tens of millions of Chinese, he did construct roads, radio stations, etc., and simplified the complex Chinese alphabet for typesetting purposes.

So guess who's going to be using all those roads and typesetting in the near future. Us, that's who.

Very roughly, there are now fifty million believers in China, counting children. In other words, for every Chinese slain by Mao, there is now at least one Christian.

Did God lose control at TienAnMen Square? According to a report in the February 3, 1990, *World,* "In at least seven cities students have indicated that as many as ten per cent of entire student bodies have converted since the June 4 massacre. In some cases entire dorms or even faculties have all become Christians."

One lecturer at Xiamen University said, "I would defy anyone to walk from one building to another on this campus and not bump into a group of students having a Bible study in the open air." Hey, if that doesn't excite you, check your pulse!

Stop the Kairos, I Want to Get Off

We're nowhere near prepared to handle the Soviet breakup opportunity. And when Red China opens, we'll be even *less* prepared to handle that one.

No surprise here, though. When MacArthur appealed to the church to send a host of missionaries to the broken and receptive people of Japan, the church yawned. And today Japan is an economic giant with a spiritual vacuum for a heart.

It looks from here like we're preparing to foul up again.

The problem is not a shortage of planning. *Glory!* Have we ever got plans!

Out of the 78 plans to evangelize the world that I mentioned before, 33 of them are backed by organizations spending over a *billion* dollars per decade.

Each.[15]

Just one gargantuan flaw in all this. Whether a plan is sponsored by a church or a parachurch organization, it's all the same. Both the outreachers and the new converts will come to the hour when the believer marches in and plops himself in a pew.

Sooner or later, every participant in every one of those brilliant plans wends his way to church. That's where the road slopes softly downward, winds through a maze of liturgical loop-de-loops, threads through a thicket of theological lint, and peters out in a pool of ecclesiastical inertia.

They walk in as plain folks, we turn 'em into an audience.

To compensate for the silence and needs and spiritual death, we have a zillion programs, from Bible studies to junior high scavenger hunts, and many of them are helpful. But as a whole these don't keep

---

[15] Barrett and Reapsome, op. cit., p. 42.

people growing long term. People plateau. *For 95% of them, spiritual growth slows to a snail shuffle within two years.* (You can quibble with these exact numbers, but in your heart you know I'm approximately right.)

The Main Point

Seems like everybody is praying for a revival for these days.

(I'll overlook the annoying fact that many revivals of the past started with a confession of sin in church, and today we don't even have a slot in the service where people could confess to overtime parking.)

My point is simple: **If we *do* see a revival, or a great ingathering of souls here or overseas, there's no way in the world we'll be able to handle it with a closed-church system where things tend to revolve around professionals.**

There's no way we'd be able to grind out seminary grads fast enough to fill the pulpits and feed the converts. We've simply got to find more feasible ways to raise up those who can minister.

There's no way we'd be able to build church buildings fast enough, either. We've already got scads of young urban churches meeting in warehouses because they can't get a building permit or a traditional church plant is too expensive to build.

There's no way we'd be able to give millions of converts a chance to lead in worship and ministry. They could never function on a regular basis or find their niche in a traditional "foundation-laying" period that would last so long it would kill their momentum. Except for celebrities, we dump all new converts into the "not ready for prime time" category. Sometimes five to ten years, sometimes forever.

That's not a speed bump, it's a penalty box. We cannot let this happen again as the east opens to us. A new approach must be found.

The Good News

Although we evangelicals are divided into mainline evangelical, Pentecostal, charismatic, fundamentalist, reconstructionist, and a few other camps, John 17 unity has overcome much of the coolness that prevailed just twenty-five years ago.

And for all those twenty-five years, we have been just beginning to tap the power of an *open* church worldwide:

- Overseas, the church is already rediscovering, in glorious bits and pieces, the secret of the explosive growth of the early church.
- The Chinese church has found a large part of it.
- Many of the Soviet "Baptist" churches used it to stay alive during the dark years.
- The roaring house-church movement in Great Britain is picking up on it. A recent seminar on worship there drew 30,000!
- Here in North America, God has transformed thousands through home gatherings, even though most do no more than dabble with it.[16]

But strangely, very few have put their fingers on exactly what is needed to transform themselves into open churches, into powerful, edifying, bodies of believers. Perhaps now that *you've* read this little booklet, that will start to change (at least in your area). Right? If nobody's looking, nod your head *yes*.

The Big Plans for the Future

As soon as participation becomes a trend we'll be playing a different ball game.

Today there are 500 million Great Commission Christians worldwide and 3.4 billion people who don't claim to be Christians at all. *That's only seven people for each true disciple!*

God plans to cross-pollenate the still-suffering church—from Bucharest to Beijing—with the rich and sophisticated western church...thus buttressing them and revitalizing us! That is His overall blueprint.

But do His plans always work out? Does God always win?

No. Thanks to His questionable taste in strategy (using humans), He often loses, *short term.* It's kind of like letting your three-year-old help you hang wallpaper.

So in the future, we could lose some big battles. No one knows exactly how much mischief the Red (and once-Red) governments may yet do. Or what unexpected things lie ahead. But the God of History will *not* lose the Great War for this Earth. He has exciting plans for the newly-free church *and* the body of believers here in North America.

---

[16] I think house churches are wonderful. If a church were to consider breaking up into a group of house churches, my advice would likely be, "Go ahead, and let the bricks fall where they may!" But realistically, I know that few traditional churches will ever choose to give up their buildings.

The New World is Approaching

Something is out there.

When the western world first became systematically unified—under the bureaucratic oppression of Caesar Augustus—it was the tripwire for the first advent, the birth of the Lord Jesus Christ.

Now we have a world on the brink of nobody knows what, with Communism in total collapse and the EC forming a whole new Europe. Surely their united Europe will not take long before it tries to become a grand Atlantic alliance with the United States... and then soon a world alliance, a "new world order."

Perhaps that alliance will be a tripwire for the Lord's Second Advent. Or perhaps that Advent will be delayed by the massive Christian bloodbath that may be required before the Arab Crescent turns to the Cross. Or perhaps some further challenge awaits. Who knows?

But whatever comes to pass, the impending cyclone of events will not allow us the leisure of a closed church. We *must* return to first century patterns. Now!

So as we sail into these uncharted seas, how greatly we need to be salt and light. How greatly we need to meet the Prince of Darkness with the *full force* of the entire church arrayed in a battle formation with each and every warrior functioning.

How greatly we need to make the lines of communication to God *and* each other open.

Now.

Better than church?
Being the church!

Marks of an Open Meeting

I **Open Worship.** You are allowed to praise and worship God, speaking with your own words and leading the gathering's thoughts and hearts during a time designated for worship. The priesthood of the believer has become a full reality at last.

II **Open Sharing.** You are free to speak on personal and spiritual matters during sharing. Modes of sharing might include confession, thanksgiving, statement of need, testimony, intercessory prayer and requests for same, reading of Scripture or literary nuggets, etc. Loneliness has begun to vanish.

III **Open Ministry.** You are encouraged to employ all your gifts and talents, both inside and outside your meetings. The wide variety of ministries includes speaking; singing; creating and managing projects you've begun; putting the church in contact with events, acts of God, and special needs worldwide; and much more. Spiritual apartheid ends.

JAMES RUTZ is president of Open Church Ministries in Costa Mesa, California, an information network designed to help churches wanting to reclaim the powerful dynamics and love of a truly biblical congregation without taking the radical step of dissolving into a cluster of house churches. The key strategies advocated are to open the worship service to full participation and to empower strong lay leadership.

As a free lance writer for eighteen difficult but rewarding years, Mr. Rutz (rhymes with klutz, he says) has divided his time 50/50 between secular writing and Christian writing. He has served or written for organizations like World Vision, Wycliffe, Youth for Christ, Prison Fellowship, Jews for Jesus, InterVarsity, Global Opportunities, and Dawn Ministries. On the secular side, he has specialized in direct response advertising, with some emphasis on finance and politics. He also consults as a fund-raiser for other ministries and speaks to churches. He is single and enjoys racquetball, running, and compulsive reading that includes forty-five periodicals.